Jim Clark

A Florida Cattle Ranch

A *F*lorida

 PINEAPPLE PRESS, INC.
Sarasota, Florida

By Alto (Bud) Adams Jr. and Lee Gramling

Cattle Ranch

Inquiries should be addressed to:
Pineapple Press, Inc.
P.O. Box 3899
Sarasota, Florida 34230

LIBRARY OF CONGRESS CATALOGING IN
PUBLICATION DATA

Adams, Alto.
A Florida cattle ranch / by Alto (Bud)
Adams Jr. and Lee Gramling. 1st ed.
      p.   cm.
ISBN 1-56164-159-6 (hardbound : alk.
paper). ISBN 1-56164-166-9
(pbk. : alk. paper)
1. Ranches—Florida.
2. Ranching—Environmental aspects—
Florida. 3. Adams, Alto.
 I. Gramling, Lee, 1942–   . II. Title.
SF196.U5A335   1998
636.2'01'09759—dc21   98–25799
                                    CIP

First Edition
10 9 8 7 6 5 4 3 2 1

Design by Carol Tornatore

Printed in Hong Kong

Table of Contents

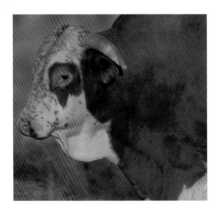

Acknowledgments

This book includes some thoughts and photographs about a part of Florida which has remained largely unchanged from earlier times. The photographs document the last ten years on Adams Ranch: what the land looked like, what wildlife lived here, and how cattle were raised.

I would like to thank Lee Gramling, who helped with gathering history and editing. The late J. R. Skaggs was office manager at Adams Ranch for many years and helped keep a record of the information in this book. Gloria Moore cataloged photos, and Diane Haenning was a great help as well. Noted wildlife photographer "Chica" Stracener assisted in arranging text on whitetail deer.

I owe special thanks to my wife Dorothy for working on the computer and patiently getting this project together. Finally, I thank the cowmen who are responsible for the care and management of the cattle: Lee Adams, Mike Adams, Buddy Adams, Ron Trythall, Billy Adams, Ralph Pfister, Frank Lewis, Rogelio Cardona, Robert Adams, Jerry Wester, and the citrus crew.

— *Bud Adams*

To every thing there is a season
and a time to every purpose.

—*Ecclesiastes 3:1*

S outh and central
Florida have experi-
enced the eternal
cycles of water, land,
and sky, life and death and
rebirth, since long before the
dawn of recorded history.
For countless aeons, our
peninsula seemed unsure
whether to exist as ocean
floor or dry ground. Volcanoes
and earthquakes, ice ages and
global warming—each in turn
altered the delicate balance
among these primal elements.

Authorities report that our
"Land of Flowers" emerged
from the sea in its present form
some twelve thousand years
ago. Yet even today the cycles
continue. The subtropical sun
evaporates water from the
surrounding ocean and our
abundant lakes and rivers to
form clouds which return it to

land as rain. This is quickly swallowed up by a porous aquifer, and the process begins anew. Flood and drought—sometimes separated from one another by only a few weeks—are as indigenous to native Florida as they are frustrating to visitors who may thoughtlessly chide Mother Nature for her lack of constancy.

With each new year, plants in Florida flower and bear fruit, and grasses grow to cover the prairies. Bees suck nectar from flowers and distribute the pollen that makes the fruit possible. Birds eat the fruit, and cattle graze on the tender grass. Their hooves break up the soil to accept new seeds which are spread by the birds. The manure of all creatures nourishes the soil.

Green plants cool the earth and generate oxygen for animals; animals produce carbon dioxide and nitrates that feed plants. The persistent rains invigorate everything, while run-off water is purified by natural filters of lime rock, sod, and sand.

When the time arrives, each animal mates and produces offspring. Predators feed upon these offspring and the weaker adults, holding populations in check and strengthening every species. Carrion-eaters and insects remove the soft tissues, and the bones remain to enrich the earth.

Life, death, rebirth: these are the timeless rhythms of the universe. Only the pride and willfulness of restless humans could aspire to improve on them, and they undertake to do so at their peril.

No one knows this better, or should know it, than those who take their living from the land. There is no science of agriculture or "agribusiness" that can render the farmer or the herdsman immune to the ebb and flow of nature's cycles. And no one has greater stake in preserving the land in its natural condition than those whose families have lived for generations with its endless change, its perpetual beauty, and its occasional cruelties.

The word for this is stewardship: a deeply-held conviction that whoever owns and uses the land merely holds it in trust for future generations.

The photographs by Bud Adams in this book reflect a lifelong love affair with the palmetto prairies, hammocks, swamps, and piney woods of south central Florida.

Alto "Bud" Adams Jr., a partner in Alto Adams and Son, has lived on Adams Ranch since he graduated from the University of Florida in 1947. The ranch covers over 50,000 acres and is in three divisions in St. Lucie, Osceola, and Okeechobee Counties, with headquarters in St. Lucie County. The ranch is also home to the Braford breed of cattle, which originated on the St. Lucie ranch with the first Brahman-Hereford crosses in 1948.

Bud Adams views his responsibility of stewardship over this unique land—some of the last truly wild country in Florida—as a sacred obligation. It's an obligation shared by his children and grandchildren.

This book was written for newcomers to our state as well as for native-born Floridians. Newcomers may see a part of Florida they hadn't seen before, and natives may remember the "old Florida" they grew up loving. It's only natural for new arrivals to feel nostalgic about the places they left behind and to be tempted to alter their new surroundings in ways that will make them seem more like "home." Yet not every change is for the better, as humans all over the world have learned to their sorrow.

Florida's complex ecology has gotten along very well without man's "help" for a long time. Perhaps all of us could benefit from a closer look at the land we live in, before plunging in precipitously with ideas to "improve" it. Perhaps this book will serve as a starting place for such a thoughtful, affectionate reconnaissance.

The *L*and

…a land fair and spacious …

—Exodus 3:8

At one time grassy prairies and pine flatwoods covered virtually all of south central Florida, from the tiny cattle town of Orlando to the shores of Lake Okeechobee, west to the Gulf of Mexico and east to the Atlantic Ocean.

Rich prairies of native wiregrass, maidencane, and wild carpet spread south along the Kissimmee and St. Johns Rivers, separated by tall forests of virgin pine. The Kissimmee River runs parallel to the St. Johns River. The St. Johns flows north to Jacksonville and the Kissimmee flows south into Lake Okeechobee. The Kissimmee prairie bordered both sides of the Kissimmee River. Cabbage palms and live oak hammocks marked fertile grassland.

The land here seldom rises more than eighty feet above sea level, and the soil is sandy and acidic. It is poor farming country but ideal for grazing the hardy cattle that have become acclimated to Florida's subtropical environment. Interspersed among the prairies and pine woods are small creeks, swamps, cypress domes, and hardwood hammocks. These are home to countless species of wildlife, as are the prairies themselves and the cabbage palm and pine hammocks which rise up among them.

Our native word "hammock" comes from an Indian expression meaning "a place of shade," and there are several varieties in Florida. When seen from a distance among miles of featureless prairie, hammocks of oak, pine, and palm trees appear to be islands in an endless sea of grass. Farther south, in the broad, slow-moving river called the Everglades, they may literally be islands, rising a few inches or feet above the surrounding wetlands.

It is this appearance perhaps which has caused newcomers to confuse our local term with the more familiar "hummock," a small rounded knoll or hill. But in Florida there are low hammocks also. These welcome refuges from the summer's heat can be found along the edges of swamps or in the flood plains of rivers. They are frequently carpeted over with fallen leaves, lending an almost reverent silence to the shaded coolness beneath thick canopies of cypress, maple, sweet gum, and bay.

Cypress domes are so-called because those ancient and distinctive trees have a tendency to grow taller at the center than around the fringes of the small patches of wetland they occupy in prairie country. Many such domes can still be seen from the relative elevation of the Florida turnpike south of Kissimmee.

Pine flatwoods might appear stark and uninteresting to the inexperienced observer, but they contain between fifty and seventy-five different species of plants per acre. They are home to the bald eagle, the red-bellied woodpecker, and the diamondback rattlesnake, among other native fauna. Various grasses grow naturally beneath the tall trees, so cattle graze here as readily as in the open prairies.

South Florida's climate is subtropical, so there are clearly defined wet and dry seasons here. The wet season starts in June and lasts through October, coinciding with the hurricane season. The rains of August, September, and October account for roughly half of the area's average annual precipitation of sixty inches.

Frederic Remington, the famous Western artist who visited our state in 1895, observed disparagingly that "all that is not mud, mud, mud is sand, sand, sand." Longtime residents are well accustomed to the frequent cycles of flood and drought. Any time the weather is wet it seems to get wetter, and when it is dry it seems to get drier.

During spring and summer the prevailing winds are from the east and south, and offshore breezes combine with almost daily showers to render the hottest months mild and humid. The rest of the year the winds are from the west and north. But although these winds bring with them occasional winter freezes, abundant water and our southern latitude combine to temper their more extreme effects.

To the east of the St. Johns River and its swampy headwaters, the land slopes down to low coastal marshes and ancient dunes. Where prehistoric shellfish have left their subterranean deposits, hardwoods take root in slightly higher tracts of less acidic soil. It is here—west of Fort Pierce bordering Cow Creek—that Adams Ranch has its headquarters.

Native *I*nhabitants

For this is the law of the jungle
As old as the sea and the sky.
And the creature that keeps it will prosper,
And the creature that breaks it shall die.

—Rudyard Kipling

*F*rom earliest times, the history of Florida has been characterized by successive waves of immigration—a seemingly endless cavalcade of newly arrived plant life, animal species, and peoples. Sometimes these have displaced the earlier inhabitants; more often they've managed to adapt and find their own niche in our richly varied environment. "Native," therefore, is at best a relative term.

There was an era when mastodons, mammoths, and saber-toothed tigers roamed the Florida peninsula, together with prehistoric horses, giant land turtles, and even camels. More recently, and for several centuries after the first Europeans arrived, buffalo were observed among the lush

7

As a small boy in the 1930s, I would visit Indian camps. Polly Parker, a survivor of the Indian wars of the middle 1850s, lived close to Polly Hammock and was said to be one hundred years old. Chief Checpo had a small garden plot in Checpo Hammock. Relics of these camps and a dugout canoe have been preserved at ranch headquarters.

— Bud Adams

grasslands and virgin pine forests. Panthers prowled our dense hammocks and sand hill scrub until the early 1930s.

Human life has existed here from early times as well. The Paleoindians who migrated south around 10,000 B.C. eventually gave way to the early, middle, and late Archaic peoples, followed by a variety of pre-Columbian cultures including the St. Johns, Deptford, Weeden Island, and Belle Glade. All of them seemed to adapt readily to their new homeland, hunting, fishing, occasionally raising small crops of corn and pumpkin, and generally living in harmony with Florida's rich, abundant ecosystem.

When the first European colonists arrived in 1564 and 1565, the principal native peoples were the Apalachee of northwest Florida, the Timucua in north and central Florida, and the fiercely independent Calusa, who exercised dominion over the southwest part of the peninsula. Along the southeastern coast were several smaller tribes, including the Ais and the Tekesta.

Unlike their counterparts in Mexico and South America, the relatively small number of Spanish settlers coexisted peacefully with the Apalachee and Timucua in Florida. Many of these natives converted to Christianity and became skilled farmers and herdsmen.

But smallpox and other European diseases, together with the depredations of northern invaders (most notably the English, who with their Creek allies ravaged the Spanish missions in 1702 and 1704), eventually decimated this "aboriginal" population and left the way open for still more waves of human immigration.

The forests and palmetto prairies of south central Florida continue to support countless species of wildlife that were here before Juan Ponce de León first peered out from his quarterdeck to give the "Land of Flowers" its name. Among these are furbearers such as the gray fox, raccoon, otter, rabbit, opossum, and whitetail deer; predators like the Florida panther, bobcat, black bear, and alligator; a variety of poisonous and nonpoisonous snakes; and a proliferation of bird life that was once so great, early visitors reported that when they took to flight they literally darkened the sky.

Sandhill cranes
in flight.

This sandhill crane is nesting in a pond. Both parents take turns raising the chicks. Generally, two eggs hatch and one chick survives.

Bird Life

Today, south Florida cattle ranches provide major sanctuaries for an abundance of feathered species, including the bald eagle, Florida sandhill crane, Osceola wild turkey, crested caracara, and many varieties of water birds such as the anhinga, Florida mallard, wood ibis, and several kinds of heron and egret.

The Florida sandhill crane, largest of all sandhill cranes, lives year-round on Florida's native prairies and marshes, unlike its northern cousins, which only winter here. This bird is very intelligent and, where it has not been molested, gentle as well. Sandhills perform a loud and graceful mating dance, accompanied by their characteristically shrill cries.

They nest in shallow ponds on piled-up grass. The young first appear as balls of orange fuzz, and when they are able to move about on their own, they follow the older birds in the open, generally in family groups of two or three. At first glance they might seem to be quite vulnerable to predators. But older birds are evidently capable of protecting their young, since sandhill cranes continue to flourish on south Florida's ranches.

Also found in large numbers on the open prairies are the beautiful-voiced mourning dove and the bobwhite quail. The snipe is a seasonal visitor, whose protective coloring blends easily with its surroundings and whose long beak is well suited to probing

Mourning dove

moist pasture land.

The Florida gallinule (common moorhen) is at home in the canals and waterways of Adams Ranch. Other water birds include the wood duck, the common egret, the snowy egret, the white ibis, the heron, and the wood stork, which is the only native American stork. Most wading birds tend to feed together and cooperate rather than compete for food.

Like the native sandhill crane, the Florida mallard (also called the mottled duck) nests and lives in our peninsular back country all year long. It resembles a female greenhead, but since it has abundant food locally and does not migrate, it tends to grow larger and plumper than its northern kin.

The anhinga is a skilled fisherman. It is also known as the "snake bird" because it typically sinks into the water with only its long, dark neck protruding. Lacking natural waterproofing for its feathers, it is frequently seen spreading its wings to dry upon nearby shrubs. Anhingas hatch three or four chicks at a time, which grow rapidly on their fish diet.

By far the most spectacular feathered predator of the Florida prairies is the American bald eagle. Keen-sighted, high-soaring, and almost constantly on the move above open country where it hunts prey and builds its nest, this large, beautiful bird is exceedingly difficult to approach and photograph. Bald eagles have established

The common moorhen, also known as the Florida gallinule, is at home on Adams Ranch.

A bobwhite quail among the myrtles

Male bobwhite quail

Once on the verge of extinction, today the wood duck is a common sight in swamplands and woodlands year-round.

The Great egret, also called the common egret (top), and the snowy egret, performing its mating dance (bottom), were hunted nearly to extinction early in this century. Both birds have made a remarkable comeback.

White ibis nest in large colonies throughout Florida from March through May.

themselves at a number of sites on Adams Ranch, building large, impressive nests which they typically use for several years before moving on to new locations. Some of them appear to migrate seasonally, while others remain in the same general area for years at a time. Their diet includes fish from Lake Marian and Lake Kissimmee, as well as a wide variety of small animals and carrion.

Other feathered predators include night-hunting owls and high-flying hawks, both of which control the local population of rodents, frogs, and snakes. The burrowing owl makes its home on the palmetto prairies, while the larger barred owl favors deep woods and swamps. The most common hawk to inhabit Florida hammocks is the red-shouldered hawk. Its range and hunting territory are limited, and it should not be confused with the red-tailed hawk, which is more often found among pine flatlands.

The turkey vulture and the crested caracara perform a crucial role in south Florida's sometimes harsh and always volatile ecosystem. These native scavengers draw their sustenance from the dead and from live animals that are in a weak or crippled state. The caracara, despite its bright plumage and ghoulish tastes, is a surprisingly gentle bird. It is easily approached by humans and has been seen to be driven from its nest by common crows.

Typically solitary birds, green-backed herons may also nest in large colonies with other green-backed herons or with other bird species.

Some green-backed herons actually fish using bait: they drop berries or insects into the water to attract minnows.

Wood storks are also called "ironheads." Due to loss of wetlands, they are now on both state and federal endangered species lists.

Anhingas are called snake birds, because often their snakelike necks are all you see protruding from the water.

Young anhingas are covered with a velvetlike fuzz.

Bald eagle

The barred owl prefers
to nest in natural holes in
hardwoods or palms.

The burrowing owl, most
common to the Kissimmee
Prairie, nests one to three feet
underground.

The crested caracara feeds on
reptiles, birds, mammals,
and carrion in pasturelands.

The red-shouldered hawk is the most common hawk found in the hammocks. Its range seems limited, and its locations are predictable. Relying on a diet of rats, frogs, and snakes, red-shouldered hawks do not seem to compete with red-tailed hawks, which are found more often on pinelands.

Like the snail kite, the limpkin depends upon the apple snail as a food source. Limpkins, however, also eat frogs, worms, insects, and crustaceans.

The Everglades kite is commonly called the snail kite and is dependent on the apple snail for food. The male, pictured here with a snail, is slate gray. The female is brown and frequently raises three or four chicks.

Swallow-tailed kites are seasonal
visitors that arrive in March and
build nests. Graceful flyers, they
have striking markings.

Top: The least bittern is at home
in the cattails.

Bottom: The American bittern
relies on stealth when hunting its
prey of frogs, fish, and assorted
invertebrates.

The roseate spoonbill has a spoon-shaped beak to feed on small organisms in mud and receding water.

Roseate spoonbills with egrets

The Firebird

The Osceola subspecies of wild turkey is found only on the Florida peninsula. A large, beautiful bird with iridescent markings, a turkey is whatever color the sunlight makes it: it may appear copper-colored and red to one observer, black, green or gray to another. It is one of nature's perfect creatures— intelligent, wary, a fast runner, and a rapid flier despite its size. For those who hunt it, either with firearm or camera, there is no greater challenge to human skill and patience.

Turkeys spend the day in open grasslands, where they can receive early warning of the presence of bobcats and other predators. They seldom range more than half a mile from trees, which afford a refuge in the event of attack and a roosting place at night. The hens are

The Osceola subspecies of wild
turkey is found nowhere else
but on the Florida peninsula.

These turkeys are seldom seen
in trees in sunlight. This turkey
had flown to roost during a dark
rainstorm and was photographed
just at sunset as the sun shone
through the clouds.

Turkey in flight.

Excerpts from Bud Adams' diary:

JANUARY 20, 1990: I noticed the first gobbler fanning and strutting at the Lake Marian Ranch today. Last year there was a large hatch of young turkeys in Osceola County. In less than one mile, it is possible to see more than one hundred turkeys. They are in groups of a hen and eight to ten young turkeys.

MARCH 30, 1997: This is late spring, gobbler season. Most of the hens have left the flock to nest. Gobblers are still active. Clover is the principal feed at this time.

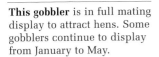

This gobbler is in full mating display to attract hens. Some gobblers continue to display from January to May.

accompanied by one or two long-bearded gobblers. The dominant gobbler will strut and gobble; his companion will remain nearby to act as lookout. This makes the flock extremely difficult to approach.

As they fly up to roost, the large birds can be seen and heard for long distances. Then they will hop among foliage and disappear from view. When they come off the roost, they sail back to earth with scarcely a sound. Hens and young turkeys roost in oaks and cabbage palms while the old gobblers prefer tall pines or cypress. Their roosts are frequently located above palmettos or water; this makes them hard to approach without betraying one's presence.

At one time, in many parts of the United States, wild turkeys were almost eliminated. This was also true in sections of north Florida. With the help of the National Wild Turkey Federation and other concerned hunters' organizations, most of these areas have now been restocked.

On the open range of south Florida, the Osceola turkey was never seriously threatened, and the birds we see today are a pure strain descended from pre-Columbian times. They are distinguished by their long legs, trim build, distinctive coloring, and the edge of their tails.

Large cattle ranches provide a perfect habitat for the turkey's continued survival. There is no major competition for its diet of acorns, cabbage berries, pasture vegetation, and gallberries. In the summer it supplements its diet with grasshoppers, worms, and a variety of insects. Grazing cattle maintain the open grassland that turkeys need in order to flourish, while fencing and posting protect them from illegal hunting.

Two whitetail bucks

The Whitetail Deer

This widespread species has become specially adapted to Florida's unique combination of food supply, heat, humidity, and predators. Smaller than its northern counterpart, the Florida whitetail deer is well suited to our warmer climate and dense vegetation.

The deer's natural foods include acorns, palmetto berries, cabbage berries, wild grapes, persimmons, and leafy browse, all of which afford good seasonal nutrition. Today on Adams Ranch, legumes such as white clover, desmodium, and deer vetch, which are planted for cattle, also sustain deer when native browse isn't available. Supplemental feeding with grain, a poor substitute for natural plant foods, modifies behavior and

When bucks are in velvet, they segregate from the does and group together.

While in velvet, they begin to establish dominance. They cannot fight with their soft horns, so they rear up and fight with their front hooves.

tends to make deer dependent and partly domesticated.

Deer are nocturnal creatures by nature. In daylight, they rely on their senses of smell and hearing more than their eyesight. When the wind is right, a person who remains still may escape their notice entirely. By moving quietly when the animal has its head down feeding, then "freezing" in place whenever it raises its head, one may often approach within a few feet without disturbing it.

In south central Florida, fawns are usually born in March and April, somewhat earlier than in the northern parts of the state. At this time of year, bucks have lost their antlers and remain separate from the does, which live in family groups composed of several generations of does and

Having shed his velvet, this buck has freshly polished antlers. His large neck indicates the beginning of the breeding season.

their offspring. Dominant does will drive away young bucks and unrelated does.

Mature does often raise twins. The does feed on young browse and clover, which is nutritious and provides milk for the fawns. Fawns stay hidden in high grass and clover until they are old enough to escape from predators. When white clover is in bloom, it makes the spotted fawns difficult to see.

Within six weeks of losing their old rack, bucks begin to form new antler growth on their stumps, or "pedicles." A buck's antlers are the fastest-growing things in the animal kingdom, increasing by as much as half an inch a day. These antlers are encased in a layer of velvet which contains blood and nutrients. By early summer, the fawns have become fat and have lost their spots, and bucks have their new antlers in velvet.

As antlers grow they harden, and soon the bucks will begin rubbing small trees and shrubs to rid their racks of the dying velvet, a sign that

Dominant does will drive away young bucks and unrelated does.

the bucks are approaching their time to breed. Soon their necks will thicken, and fat they have gained from summer eating will turn to muscle. Testosterone levels rise, and they begin seeking receptive does.

Antlers are status symbols of male prowess and virility. Stronger bucks with larger antlers will be able to attract and defend a greater number of does. This process of natural selection enhances survival and enables the entire species to become stronger.

During September in south central Florida, all deer become very active. At first a doe will dash around a group of other does to attract attention to herself. Normally nocturnal bucks will appear in broad daylight and attach themselves to a group of does. Bucks will begin fighting among themselves to establish dominance. These contests of strength are violent and may result in crippling injuries or even death.

In St. Lucie County, fawns are usually born in March and April. Further north in Florida, fawns are born later.

By the time the rut is over, many bucks have lost as much as twenty percent of their body weight due to the rigors of the mating season. Even with the relative abundance of food in Florida's lush subtropical environment, most bucks begin the new year with a ragged appearance. But soon the clover will once more be in bloom, new fawns will be born, and the cycle will start all over again.

Florida's deer have survived screwworms, overhunting, lack of food, and loss of habitat. The result is an ideal example of nature's shaping an animal to suit its environment. Those which remain are straight-backed and well muscled, with fine legs and excellent antlers. Each one is a perfect deer.

Fawns hide in grass and clover until they are old enough to escape predators.

SEPTEMBER 10, 1997: *I've noticed that when feed is plentiful, deer do not move long distances. Does remain in their feeding area, and bucks seek them out. A buck driven from one locale will seek another.*

Large herds of deer will gather when summer legumes are good.

Cattle and deer are compatible on the open range, because cattle are grazers and deer are browsers. Where there are many cattle and few deer, trees and brush encroach on the grasslands. Where there are deer and no cattle, the grass accumulates and wildfires destroy trees. Deer consume relatively little grass, but they eat clover and summer legumes along with the cattle. The best summer legumes are aschenomyne, commonly called deer vetch, and desmodium.

The pastures of Adams Ranch must be limed every three or four years in order to sustain the clover and other legumes. Phosphorus and potash are also added, along with additional nutrients that may be suggested by soil tests. The large numbers of whitetail deer which live on the ranch provide a reliable indicator of soil conditions. Since deer require a greater protein content than cattle, one of the first signs that a pasture is declining is the migration of deer to a better food source. If they're unable to find one, their physical condition will decline and poor antlers will result.

A successful deer management program must take into account both good nutrition and improved genetics. Extensive acreage is needed to support abundant populations with a broad genetic base, which prevents inbreeding and maintains the overall vigor of the species. By supporting deer on their open range, larger Florida ranches play a vital role in promoting biodiversity.

On Adams Ranch, deer

herds are periodically evaluated and doe permits are obtained when it becomes necessary to restore proper buck-to-doe ratio. If the deer population is too numerous to be sustained on existing feed, limited hunting of does is allowed. Whenever herd size needs to be increased, doe hunting is prohibited. The key to deer management is the number of breeding females.

One fact is clear in all aspects of animal husbandry, including the management of wildlife: the combination of genetics, natural selection, and human guidance will determine the kinds of animals we have. Normal evolution may take centuries to alter a species. Yet on Adams Ranch, where cattlemen have limed the land, overseeded grass with legumes, posted the property, and enforced controlled hunting, deer have become larger and more prolific in just thirty-five years.

Diamondback rattlesnake

Florida Predators

Predators are nature's way of enforcing population balance and genetic selectivity among many species. Just as the eagle, owl, and hawk control the numbers of rodents, frogs, and snakes in Florida's prairies and hammocks, native hunters such as bobcats, otters, raccoons, and alligators thin the populations and strengthen the genetic adaptability of rabbits, birds, turkeys, and other species.

The Florida bobcat is a large cat, growing to about the size of a German Shepherd dog. It is very near the top of the natural food chain and thrives on the plentiful supply of rabbits, rodents, turkeys, and small deer found on south Florida ranches. Like its distant cousin the Florida panther, it typically covers its kill with leaves and grass in order to return for later feeding.

Bobcats are nocturnal hunters, and adult cats are seldom seen in daylight. In the morning, their tracks are easily found where they have prowled the ranch's cow trails and dirt roads. Young cubs can sometimes be observed playing near their dens, but the dens themselves are difficult to locate.

If the bobcat is a top predator on land, the otter is the master predator in the water. Its active lifestyle requires huge quantities of fish to sustain it. Once seriously threatened by trappers who coveted its sleek pelt, the otter presently thrives in south Florida's wetlands.

These bobcats were photographed at a fresh deer carcass that they had partially eaten and then covered with grass so vultures wouldn't disturb it.

Otters

Raccoons are also plentiful, now that they are no longer hunted for their skins. They are omnivorous and will eat virtually anything humans eat. Their diet includes fish, crayfish, small animals, fruits, vegetables, and anything else their active feet can find.

Another species once driven to the brink of extinction by uncontrolled hunting is the Florida alligator. It has made a striking recovery since the 1930s, and as the gator population has increased, there has been a corresponding decrease in the number of moccasins, water snakes, and various other creatures, including substantial quantities of fish, in some Florida lakes.

The alligator has no natural enemies apart from man. It will eat nearly anything, including fish, frogs, turtles, snakes, birds, and mammals. If its numbers increase to the point of outstripping the food supply, it readily turns to cannibalism in order to satisfy its voracious need for protein.

When attacking its prey, an alligator's mouth clamps shut with tremendous force, easily crushing the bones of even very large animals. The muscles which open the mouth are relatively weak, however, allowing skilled gator hunters (and those who "wrestle" the reptiles for show) to hold them closed with surprising ease.

Raccoon

The gray fox is native to southern Florida. He has a rich, gray-colored coat with red markings.

Alligators build large nests of dirt and vegetation in which females lay their eggs. The surrounding temperature helps determine the sex of newly hatched gators. Young hatchlings quickly seek out water and are already capable at birth of feeding on small fish and frogs. Though lacking the same maternal instincts as warm-blooded species, female alligators do tend to be protective of their young and will remain near their nests until all the baby gators are hatched.

The only limitations on an alligator's size appear to be time and available food supply. Eight- to ten-foot gators are not uncommon, and they have been known to reach lengths of sixteen feet or more.

Florida is also home to a wide variety of snakes, all of which perform the vital

A **bull alligator** bellowing. Alligators have made a rapid recovery in numbers since the 1930s.

function of controlling rodents and other pests. While most of these are perfectly harmless to humans, our state does contain several species which are, as old-time Crackers would say, "a caution."

The Florida diamondback rattlesnake is one of the largest poisonous reptiles in the world. It frequently grows to a length of eight feet, and sometimes considerably longer. Having no need to hibernate like its northern brethren, the diamondback feeds and grows year-round on our subtropical southern peninsula. Its large, triangular head and prominent fangs are enough to have a chilling effect on anyone who unwittingly intrudes upon its privacy. If the fangs are lost,

Alligators can grow very large
and can strike with great
force.

Alligators build large nests made of dirt and vegetation.

they're quickly replaced by "backup" fangs underneath the originals. The diamondback can be found almost anywhere in Florida but is especially fond of dense palmetto thickets which provide both ample cover and a regular supply of rabbits and rodents.

The cottonmouth water moccasin inhabits Florida's wetlands, streams, and rivers. Generally black or olive brown in color, it takes its name from the white puffy flesh lining the inside of its mouth, which, when opened wide with fangs extended, is a fearsome sight indeed. Moccasins can become quite broad in girth, but they seldom exceed four feet in length. Slightly less venomous than their distant cousin the rattlesnake, they tend to make up for this deficiency with an irritable, aggressive temperament.

A female alligator will remain near her nest until her young—of whom she is protective—are hatched.

Newcomers

*One generation passes
and another generation cometh,
but the land abideth forever.*

—Ecclesiastes 1:4

When fifteenth- and sixteenth-century European explorers and colonists made their first forays into the New World, they brought with them Old World flora and fauna. Among the earliest of these were orange trees, horses, swine, and long-horned cattle.

The Spanish were well aware of the cause and cure for the dreaded shipboard disease scurvy, but instead of the limes which gave English sailors their well-known nickname, the dons used oranges—originally brought into Iberia by Moslem conquerors—as their source of Vitamin C and citric acid. To provide their far-flung navy with a ready supply of the perishable fruit, they planted seeds everywhere their ships made landfall. Wild orange trees flourished in Florida's sandy acidic soil and soon spread throughout the peninsula.

Horses and hogs—the former, a form of transportation and the latter, a source of fresh meat—made their entry with de Soto, Ponce de León, Cabeza de Vaca, and other early explorers. Inevitably, some of these creatures found freedom in the lush, untrammeled Florida wilderness.

The hogs, half wild already, evolved into Florida's distinctive and fierce breed of "piney woods rooter." Escaped horses also multiplied rapidly, in part due to the Spanish aversion to gelding their riding stock.

Adams Ranch horses

Herds of wild horses were reported in parts of North America as early as the mid-1600s.

Although it has been speculated that those early conquistadors introduced beef cattle as well, their first documented arrival was in August of 1565, when Spanish colonists under Pedro Menendez de Aviles unloaded two hundred heifers—many of them carrying calves—from his ships at the newly established city of St. Augustine.

By 1600 there were thirty-four ranches in Florida with some twenty thousand head of cattle under Spanish control, not counting those captured and partly domesticated by the local Native Americans. Ranching and beef production have been central to Florida's heritage for almost four and a half centuries. Even today, with subdivisions, shopping malls, and tourist attractions making daily inroads into the peninsula's once-vast tracts of open range, we still rank tenth in number of beef cows among cattle-producing states in the country.

Relatively few immigrants came to Florida during its first two hundred years of European occupation. Beyond establishing a series of far-flung and sparsely populated ranches and missions, the Spanish had no particular interest in settling their North American possession. It's been said that the British accomplished more in this regard during their brief twenty-year tenure (from 1763 to 1783) than the Spanish did in the entire two centuries preceding it.

Cabbage palms in full bloom.

Custard apple

When the Spanish departed, along with their few hundred remaining Christianized Native Americans, the way was left open not only for settlement from across the Atlantic, but for increasing numbers of displaced persons from north of the St. Marys River. These included in particular the Seminole Indians and the British-descent frontiersmen who came to be known as "Crackers."

The tide of new arrivals had become overwhelming by the end of the American Revolution, when the English ceded Florida back to Spain. And it was only a matter of time—hastened by Napoleon's brutal invasion of their homeland—

before outnumbered Spaniards yielded to the inevitable, and Florida became a U.S. Territory. The transfer of flags occurred in 1821. Already the Seminole and Cracker cultures were well established in an uneasy but largely peaceful coexistence.

The word "Seminole" has been translated variously as "Those Who Live Apart," "Separatist," "Renegade," and "Wild People." It is said to have been originally applied by more settled members of the Creek nation to those stubbornly independent and self-sufficient Lower Creeks who chose to migrate to Florida and set up housekeeping away from the Upper Creek

Wild grapes grow in the hammocks.

tribes. Once here, they mingled with and incorporated into their culture a number of displaced peoples, including escaped slaves and the Yamasee from South Carolina. They built towns, planted crops, hunted, fished, and became some of the most skilled and productive Florida cattlemen.

The clash between Seminoles and settlers from Georgia and the Carolinas led to the Seminole Wars. Andrew Jackson, Florida's first governor, was responsible for moving many Seminoles to the West. Native Americans' cattle and crops were seized, their numbers were decimated by combat and forced relocation, and the few remaining survivors were compelled to take refuge in the desolate and forbidding swamps of the southern peninsula. Indian territory was roughly marked as south of the line of forts: Pierce, Drum, Basinger, Meade, and Myers.

The Florida Seminoles never did surrender to U.S. forces, although they finally agreed to a peace treaty in 1937. At about the same time, they began returning to their once beloved occupation of raising and breeding cattle.

In their freedom of spirit, self-sufficiency, and stubborn resistance to authority, the Seminoles were not very different from those Cracker pioneers with whom they traded, fought, and most of the time peacefully coexisted on the Florida frontier.

"These crackers," wrote Florida's Spanish Governor Vicente Manuel Zespedes in 1783, "are nomadic like Arabs and are distinguished from savages only in their color, language, and the superiority of their depraved cunning and untrustworthiness." They were, he went on to observe disdainfully, "enemies of all civil control" who "give obedience to their mother republic only when they feel like it."

As with most expressions of cultural bias, Governor Zespedes' remarks perhaps say more about his own prejudice than about those increasingly numerous arrivals from the English-speaking colonies. However, there was likely an element of truth in his assertions: even today, descendants of Crackers in rural Florida, Georgia, and Alabama are noted for their stubborn independence and taciturn resistance to change that others might interpret as downright orneriness.

They were mostly of Celtic ancestry, with a rich heritage of customs, traditions, and culture imported from England and Scotland. They migrated to Florida from Georgia and the Carolinas, where their families had begun settling several generations earlier. (The largest early influx of Scots into that area occurred in the fall of 1700, when a hurricane struck Charleston and wrecked a fleet of ships carrying colonists to Nova Scotia. The stranded survivors moved inland and settled, thus forming the foundations of many notable Southern families.) Such Florida place

The Adams Family were Southern farmers who raised cotton, corn, sweet potatoes, and cattle in Walton County, Florida, when Alto Adams Sr. was born in 1899. The wife of Alto Adams Sr. was Carra Williams from the large Williams family, who were cattlemen and hunters. Both families had migrated from Virginia through Georgia to Florida.

The Williams family sailed to Virginia from Portsmouth, England, in 1635. Adams family records were lost when Georgia courthouses were burned in the War Between the States.

names as Calhoun County, Sumter County, and Brooksville still attest to early pioneers' South Carolina roots. The Scottish influence can also be seen in many aspects of local culture, from the branding and earmarking of cattle to the "traditional" costume of the Seminole Indians, which is in fact derived from the Highlander's kilt, leggings, tartan, and tam.

Raising cattle came as naturally to these Scottish immigrants as catching fish and distilling homemade whiskey. A number of those who relocated to Florida brought their own animals with them. Some found it more convenient to start or expand their herds by appropriating livestock from Native Americans or other early residents. In any event, it was ranching that sustained many of Florida's pioneer families throughout the nineteenth century.

As the Seminoles were pushed farther and farther south toward the swampy tip of the peninsula, the ranchers followed, seeking open range that was free from the encroachment of plantations and fenced-in farms. Often they moved several times, from the swamps and piney woods of the panhandle, to the hilly scrub country of central Florida, and finally to the vast open grasslands bordering the Kissimmee River and spanning the peninsula from Bradenton and Arcadia to Fort Pierce.

The settlers' names included Adams, Albritton, Alderman, Barber, Bass, Boney, Bronson,

When houses were needed, trees were cut. Raw cowhide and buckskin held things together. Corn and sweet potatoes were staples, and beef, pork, venison, and fish provided protein. Cane supplied syrup for sweetening. Cows were penned to get manure to fertilize crops.

Carlton, Collier, Hendry, Holmes, Kempfer, Lykes, Mizell, Morgan, Overstreet, Parker, Partin, Pearce, Peeples, Platt, Raulerson, Smith, Tucker, Williams, and Yates. They transported their families and household goods in covered wagons, walking or riding alongside with a keen eye out for danger and a rifle or shotgun within easy reach, just as their counterparts did in the far West.

They built houses and barns of heart pine and cypress, strong enough to withstand hurricanes and practically immune to wet rot and termites. They erected churches and schools, and hired teachers to educate their children. They came to the Florida frontier to stay. Every one of the families mentioned has descendants in Florida, and

many continue to be involved in the cattle business.

Florida's cowmen developed their own distinctive style over the years, and they take as much pride in their catch dogs, cow whips, and sturdy Cracker ponies as their Western contemporaries do in the big-rowelled spurs, silver concho hatbands, mustangs, and lariats that have become a part of our national mythology.

The word "cowboy" wasn't used in Florida until fairly recently. Instead, those who faced the challenging task of hunting wild cows in thick hammocks and palmetto scrub were known as "cow hunters." (What was referred to as a "round-up" in the West was called a "cow hunt" locally.) Old-timers still view the term "cowboy" with a certain disdain, pointing out that in Florida it takes a man to do this kind of work, and no "boys" need apply.

The word "cowman," now as then, refers to a producer (a "rancher," in Western parlance) who raises, breeds, and sells cattle to a stocker or a feeder. In antebellum Florida, the legal definition of "cowman" was any person who owned at least eighteen head of cows, steers, bulls, or oxen. "Cattleman" is a broader term, applied to anyone who engages in any aspect of the cattle business, including stocker-grazers, feedlot operators, order buyers, commodity brokers, meat packers, and so on.

Dense hammocks and Florida's subtropical climate determined the tools of the nineteenth-century cow hunter's trade. Lariats amid thick underbrush and low hanging branches would have been about as practical as snow skis in the desert. Instead, the cow hunter used a ten- to twelve-foot cow whip and well-disciplined catch dogs to flush the cattle from cover and move them to strategically placed cow pens, where they could be branded, castrated, or simply held together until it was time to start a drive. The cow whip, whose loud crack could be heard for miles, also served as a means of communication, and in some instances, as a very formidable short-range weapon.

After the Civil War, many cow hunters preferred to use McClelland saddles rather than the heavier Western type. Their open centers were cooler for both horse and rider, while

There are several opinions about the origin of the term "cracker." *Florida cattlemen used long cow whips to drive their herds, to use as signals, or to kill rattlesnakes. Their riflelike "crack" could be heard for miles.*

the absence of a saddle horn posed little inconvenience to the drover who seldom used a lariat. Ponchos, often home-made by cutting a hole in a four-by-six-foot blanket, were favored over nonporous rubber slickers in Florida's muggy climate. And floppy-brimmed slouch hats—though perhaps not as aesthetically appealing as the Texan's ten-gallon sombrero—offered a maximum of protection against sun, rain, and insects.

As the above might suggest, the Florida cow hunter had little of the "romantic flair" of his Western counterpart, and that sometimes led visitors like artist Frederic Remington to make disparaging comparisons. But there was no tougher, more capable frontiersman. The Cracker cow hunter's clothing and equipment were

simply a reflection of his prac-tical, no-nonsense approach to the stern requirements of everyday life.

The next great wave of human migration into Florida began after the Civil War, when Northerners, attracted by our genial climate and the business and political opportunities afforded by Reconstruction, started settling with their families along the peninsula's coasts and major waterways.

As Henry Flagler's railroad extended south to St. Augus-tine in 1885, then on to Day-tona, Palm Beach, and the tiny village of Miami by 1896, the numbers of new arrivals swelled accordingly. By the start of the twentieth century, Florida's population had

Like the cow hunter and the long-horned cattle he managed, Florida's native Cracker horse earned a well-deserved reputation for toughness and the ability to survive in one of North America's most demanding environments.

Descended like the cattle from hardy Spanish stock, the Cracker horse is shaggy-maned, wiry, and small—often no more than fourteen hands high—yet remarkably durable, highly intelligent, endowed with natural "cow sense," and sure-footed among the bogs and palmetto prairies of the peninsula's treacherous back country. Many have a natural running walk, and some, a singlefoot gait known by Crackers as a "coon rack."

The stamina of Cracker horses is legendary. They would regularly put in a full day's work with their riders, from "can't see to can't see." Long strings of remounts, or remudas, were unknown on Florida cattle drives.

increased more than fivefold in less than forty years.

Additional impetus for expansion was provided by the Florida land boom of the 1920s, the huge influx of military personnel during World War II, and subsequent postwar prosperity that made our population the fastest growing in the nation for more than three decades. Today, although we rank only twenty-second among all fifty states in land area, we have become the fourth largest in number of residents.

It's a far cry from those pioneering days of the 1860s, when the entire population of present-day Brevard, Indian River, St. Lucie, and Martin Counties numbered just 246 persons, with 32 cattle for every inhabitant.

☙

Not all newcomers to Florida during the past four centuries have been human, of course, or merely those domesticated plants and animals imported by humans. A large number of wild species have arrived and taken up residence in our accommodating environment, with or without the unwitting aid of humans.

Many of these, like the red fox, cattle egret, and whooping crane, have found a comfortable niche in our state's ecology. Others, like the armadillo, coyote, fire ant, and "love bug," have been more troublesome. Still others have posed dramatic and expensive threats to the existing ecology: the Texas tick and the screwworm, which between them nearly destroyed

Cowboys on horseback

This red fox, along with the coyote, is a newcomer. Both are thriving in Florida and will probably displace some native species.

Florida's cattle industry during the early decades of this century; the Mediterranean fruit fly that ravages our citrus; the water hyacinth that stubbornly clogs our waterways; and the recently arrived and rapidly spreading Brazilian pepper and Australian melaleuca trees.

Limiting or reversing this continued influx of new arrivals, though at times wistfully dreamed of by old-timers, is not only impractical in the twenty-first century—it is frankly impossible. The best we can hope for is that each person who makes his or her home here will take time to develop a fuller understanding and appreciation of Florida's native ecology, and will accept the obligation of stewardship over this unique environment: a willingness to live with, rather than rail against, its natural cycles of storm, rain, drought, growth, death, decay, and rebirth, and to coexist in harmony with its nonhuman inhabitants.

Adams Ranch

He hath made everything beautiful in his time.

—Ecclesiastes 3:11

Adams Ranch is not old as family ranches go. It was begun in 1937 when Alto Adams Sr. began buying acreage in St. Lucie County. Until that time the land had never been fenced or developed in any way. Its only prior use had been by Native Americans, hunters, and open-range cattlemen. It was one of the last natural frontiers in the United States.

It took a man of foresight, courage, and vision to undertake such a venture in the midst of the Great Depression: foresight to recognize the potential of wild country many others considered worthless; courage to borrow the money necessary to buy the land; and optimistic vision and

The reason for the existence of Adams Ranch is grass. With the help of Florida's gentle climate, the sandy soil grows grass year-round. Since grass can't be eaten by humans, it's converted by Braford cattle into choice beef and excellent breeding stock.

This business and way of life have been built on hard work and the sandy soil. Money was borrowed to buy the land on which we raise cattle. The cattle were sold to pay for the land.

This herd of Braford cows is being rotationally grazed.

Herding cattle

level-headed determination to see an enterprise through until it ultimately succeeded. Such a man was Alto Adams Sr.

From 1948 to 1963, Alto Adams Sr. and Alto Adams Jr. bought more land and expanded their herds. In 1963, Adams Ranch was incorporated to ensure the survival of the business from one family generation to the next. Three sons of Alto Adams Jr.—Lee, Michael, and Robert—joined the ranch full time as they finished school. Elaine Harrison, Alto Adams Jr.'s sister, moved to the ranch with three of her sons. Today, thirty-one members of the family live on Adams Ranch, and the third generation is responsible for its management while the fourth generation gains hands-on experience by working cattle

during breaks from school.

Adams Ranch headquarters is located in St. Lucie County. The land is twenty-five to twenty-eight feet above sea level and consists primarily of improved pasture among hammocks. Its western boundary is Cow Creek, which contains a large stand of ancient cypress trees. The Lake Marian Ranch—purchased in three tracts between 1957 and 1963—fronts Lake Marian in Osceola County and consists mostly of open grassland on the Kissimmee Prairie, fifty miles from the home ranch. Additional tracts in Okeechobee County contain prairies and sloughs interspersed with hammocks and pine islands.

In 1937 the land looked much as it does today, though there were no fences, roads, canals, or water control then.

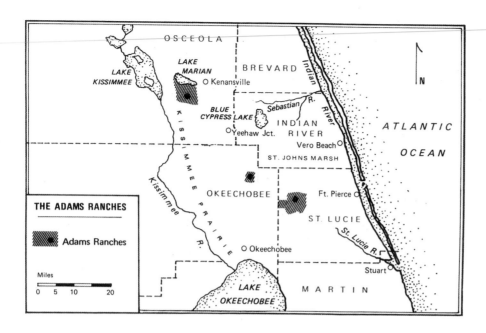

Wildlife was relatively scarce as a result of overhunting and various other threats. Cholera had killed most of the hogs. Screwworms attacked cattle, deer, and any other creature that had the misfortune to suffer a scratch or break in its hide. The Texas tick was being brought under control but was not yet completely eradicated. Malaria was still a common ailment among humans, while alternating periods of drought and flood made life for all species unpredictable at best. Fully-grown Spanish cows weighed only five hundred pounds apiece.

Improvements to the ranch were not planned: they came about in response to what sometimes appeared to be a never-ending succession of problems. There were floods, so drainage ditches were dug. There were droughts, so reservoirs were created. The grass was poor and the soil infertile, so better grass was planted, and clover and legumes were added to enrich the soil. Native cattle were too rangy and European stock were too vulnerable to south Florida's harsh environment, so the Braford breed was developed to establish a profitable balance of size, hardiness, quality, and heat tolerance.

Today Adams Ranch is a cow-calf operation that produces nearly seven thousand calves annually. The cows graze on fifty thousand acres of native and improved pasture land, and hundreds of species of wildlife flourish in harmony with the cattle.

Zachary Adams, fourth
generation

This calf's weaning weight can be predicted as 750 pounds at eight months of age, because his sire and grandsire were also that weight at that age. At maturity, he will look like the bull below.

In many respects the ranch is self-sufficient. Cows are supported entirely by available pasture: there's no need for supplemental feeding. All replacement bulls and females come from the Braford herd, which has been closed for nearly forty years. This protects the herd from the introduction of disease or genetic defects, and it allows those cattle that are best suited to Florida's environment to stand out and be selected to sire the next generation of calves.

A band of brood mares furnishes the horses that herd the cattle. They are sorrel quarter horses that have become acclimated to the subtropical climate. Red horses are preferred, because they appear to be more tolerant of the heat and free of skin diseases.

Special dogs are also raised to work the cattle. Such yellow "cur dogs" have been bred for years by Florida cattle families. They are self-reliant and hardy, and their short hair is well adapted to our heat and humidity. They're also highly intelligent, with the natural instincts required to manage cattle. Occasionally a dog may nip at a cow's legs, but it never bites hard enough to break the skin. Dogs that strip ears are not kept.

Advances in modern technology are used in the cattle industry. Bulls are production tested and semen is analyzed. Ultrasound is used to evaluate muscling and carcass value. Cattle sales are made by satellite, and computers generate daily reports on finances. Yet many day-to-day operations on the range have changed very

Most cattle are bred in multiple-sire herds. This allows bulls to establish dominance and ensures the next generation will be sired by sound bulls with strong libidos.

This cow lost her eyes shortly after birth. She was never brought to the pens, branded, or given any shots or medication. She raised calves for over twenty-six years and died on the range.

Weaned calves are being trained to herd by Lee Adams with the help of a buckskin cow whip.

little since the 1880s. Cattle are still worked by men on horseback with the help of cow dogs. The tools of the trade—spurs, saddles, cow whips, and the more recently adopted lariat—are those which were used in Florida and in the West 150 years ago. The men, too, are of that same tough breed that populated the nineteenth-century cow camps.

Where possible, the old methods have been retained on Adams Ranch because they still work and because they represent our heritage. As Alto Adams Sr.'s great-grandchildren pursue their hands-on education in the cattle business, these horses, cow dogs, and traditional equipment help to make the hard work more interesting.

There have been other improvements during the past

sixty years as well. One great improvement was the gooseneck trailer. This enabled men and horses to ride to work, saving time and allowing the men to return home each day rather than camp on the ranch. But for the most part, these changes have been made with careful consideration for their ongoing effects not only on human convenience and cattle productivity, but on all the other species that share our environment.

Natural selection, biological control, and production testing are employed to shape the Adams Ranch cattle and pasture program. Ditches distribute water and afford drainage during the wet season. Water reservoirs relieve flood runoff on the ranch and adjacent areas and create a natural breeding

Horses can go where no vehicles can. Men on horseback can handle cattle with a minimum of stress.

ground for fish, which in turn sustain eagles, ospreys, and a multitude of wading birds. The wading birds make their nests in trees around the reservoirs, where alligators help to protect their eggs and young from raccoons and other predators. Since alligators don't climb trees, the birds are comfortable with this symbiotic arrangement.

Regular soil testing and addition to the soil of calcium and phosphorus have increased the productivity of south Florida's sandy prairie country. Clover and other legumes have been planted— along with grasses such as pangola, bahia, and bermuda— to render the graze more nutritious and to increase the soil's fertility as well. As already noted, these improvements benefit deer as well as cattle.

In parts of the state where wiregrass was the principal feed for livestock, fire was historically an important feature of land management. It removed dense foliage and dead grass, allowing fresh growth to appear that was more nutritious to cattle. On Adams Ranch, fire is used very sparingly. The coexistence of cattle and deer on the same range serves to control unwanted plant growth, while improved grasses render the use of fire unnecessary and in fact destructive. The elimination of controlled burning also helps to improve air quality and to help retain organic matter in the soil.

Biological control is another means of keeping the environment healthy and self-sustaining. Birds on Adams Ranch consume pasture pests and troublesome insects, thus eliminating the need for most pesticides. Waterways support fish, which eat mosquito larvae. Hawks, owls, and other predators control the rabbit, rodent, and snake populations.

The entire history of civilization can be traced through the interaction of humans and animals. For centuries, man has hunted and followed his herds of cattle and his flocks of goats and sheep. Without these grazing animals, not only would we be deprived of meat, butter, cheese, and leather goods, but the land itself would suffer. The manure of these creatures fertilizes the ground and redistributes plant seeds. Their hooves break up the earth and create tiny collection pots for water. Their grazing forestalls the proliferation of dead grass that fuels wildfire which can destroy both trees and organic matter in the soil. The rich topsoil of the Great Plains was formed by the grazing of bison for ages. Today cattle play the same role.

From our nation's beginnings, cattle ranches have been a vital and integral part of its economy and ecosystem. They produce food for human consumption, taxes to support roads and schools and government, and a protected refuge for many kinds of wildlife. Their open range provides the greenbelts so essential to balance the pollution and environmental contamination brought about by our expanding cities and our automobiles.

The rancher or cowman

The men who oversee the cattle on Adams Ranch.

supports a huge and uniquely American industry consisting of livestock markets, order buyers, stocker-grazers, feed lot operators, meat packers, commodity brokers, and supermarket owners. In financial terms, these make up the greatest segment of our national food industry. Almost all these allied businesses make money every year,

The cattle business is simple: You breed the best to the best. You cull severely. Like begets like. You keep plenty of grass and use good bulls. Keep it simple.

—Bud Adams

though the cowman profits only about seven years out of every ten. Yet none of it can happen until the cowman produces a calf.

The nature of the cattle business has always been one of rhythms, seasons, and cycles. When the grass is green, cows are bred; nine months later, calves are born. In three more months, cows are bred again, and it is the beginning of a new season. Cattle become profitable and herds are increased; then beef prices drop, herds are liqui- dated, and prices get even worse. As cattle become scarce, prices go up again. This is the cattle cycle.

The only certainty is the certainty of change.

By **sifting through** thousands of cattle, . . .

one superior animal can be produced . . .

The Cattle Breeder

*T**he breeder is a producer** of seedstock cattle. He provides the bulls for the cowman and is responsible for the type of cattle the industry produces in the future. Traditionally, the breeder is a producer of purebred registered cattle which meet the requirements of a breed association.*

Cattle can be shaped by the eye of the breeder, just as a sculptor produces a work of art from a block of lifeless stone. Selection is the key to good versus bad, beautiful versus ugly, efficient versus wasteful. The goal of Adams Ranch has been to breed useful, productive cattle suited to a hot, humid climate.

Selection is based on weight gain by age, early maturation, good bones, and thick muscling. Cattle with pigmented eyes are retained in order to eliminate cancer eye. Those with short hair are chosen because they are more tolerant of heat, humidity, and insects.

In the spring, calves are branded and cows are dewormed. In the fall, calves are weaned. Steer calves are shipped to feed lots or to winter grazing in other parts of the United States. Calves are weighed, and heifer calves are selected for replacements. Bulls are removed from the breeding herds after the spring breeding season and are semen checked and culled before being returned to the cows the following January.

Replacement cows are retained only from those females that have had no calving difficulties. All the cattle on Adams Ranch are born without human assistance; this results in improved stock which are easier to care for and less expensive to maintain. Genetics has replaced surgery in guaranteeing healthy cattle.

who will multiply into hundreds of thousands of better cattle.

Stewardship

And if you have been faithful in that which is another's, who shall give you that which is your own?

—Luke 9:12

South Florida's coastal cities have continued to grow at a fantastic rate, especially following the widespread proliferation of air conditioning in the 1950s and '60s.

Asphalt and concrete have replaced native grass and ground cover, spreading out over the porous earth like a macadam blanket. Hardwood hammocks have been paved and landscaped; wetlands have been drained and filled; pine flatlands have been bulldozed to make way for sprawling subdivisions. Thousand-year-old cypress trees have yielded their place in the sky to postmodern spires of concrete, steel, and glass.

Millions of new human residents contribute millions of tons of sewage and solid waste to the environment every year.

Millions of automobiles generate additional pollutants, along with burgeoning industries and power plants, which, despite constant expansion, seem barely able to keep up with our swelling population's thirst for electricity. Air conditioners, though important in making life tolerable amid subtropical metropolitan sprawl, aggravate the problem. They don't manufacture cool air; they simply move it from one place to another. Their millions of sweltering exhausts transfer heat from indoors to outdoors, where it is captured and retained by the ubiquitous concrete and plaster and pavement.

Wishful thinking and nostalgic sentiment aside, there's little chance our present rate of growth will be substantially slowed—let alone reversed—in the foreseeable future. Every year the population of the United States increases by more than Florida's total number of inhabitants. Here, as in other parts of the nation, the powerful forces of human population growth are in conflict with our need for clean air and water, agriculture and food production, wildlife conservation, and recreational opportunities.

The answer to this dilemma has been known for decades yet is often overlooked in the frantic scramble to satisfy ever-increasing demands by urban residents for more technical forms of infrastructure such as roads, commercial venues, and electric power. But it is a vital aspect of infrastructure in its own right—one that lies outside the cities and seats of

Various forms of wildlife—for example, an anhinga, turtle, and alligator—can live together harmoniously.

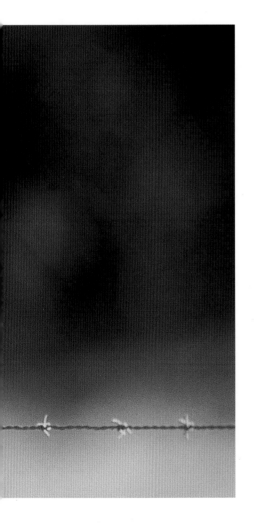

government, in those intervening greenbelts that are as essential to the survival of the cities as the improvements just mentioned.

Greenbelts are desperately needed to recycle waste, to provide watersheds and natural water purification, and to clean the atmosphere. They can and should include wilderness areas where possible, but as a matter of realistic necessity the greatest proportion must be devoted to agriculture. Pure wilderness, after all, cannot produce food to support a growing population.

In order to ensure a healthy, sustainable environment, there must be a balance between plant life and animal life. The city that has no grass or trees cannot replenish oxygen in the air. It has no way to cool its streets and buildings. Its paved-over confines inhibit the natural filtration of rainwater and replenishment of the underground aquifer. The good city must have growing things to make it livable.

A ranch will support only so many cattle, and its range, only so many deer. Any given geographic area will support only so many people, or their quality of life will suffer. An area's environment must be viewed in its entirety. Nothing less than a holistic approach can ensure that all its various elements coexist and are mutually supportive, so none infringes in harmful ways on the others. The overall picture must include humans, wildlife, vegetation, livestock, and industry. Anything that affects one of these will inevitably bring change to the rest.

The future of our cities depends on recycling waste. The continued survival of our farms and ranches requires that we use and recycle these wastes in ways which will feed and sustain cities. This is a principle Europeans have developed and fostered over centuries of population growth, and it is one they practice successfully today.

Another key to preserving our environment is biological control. Insects have developed resistance to pesticides, and bacteria have become immune to antibiotics. In fact, insects and bacteria play a vital role in our ecology, as do most other creatures if they are intelligently managed rather than rigidly controlled. Bees and butterflies pollinate crops,

feed birds, and add beauty to the landscape; soil bacteria produce nitrogen that supports plant life. Some species of bugs help control water hyacinths. Birds eat pasture pests. Fish control mosquito larvae, while mosquito hawks and martins consume adult mosquitoes. Wasps control citrus pests. Owls and hawks keep the rat, rabbit, and snake populations within bounds.

Positive environmental measures which reward conservation have proven to be effective and economically viable if they are properly structured. One is even led to suspect that perhaps Mother Nature knows better than humans how to maintain the best ecological balance.

There can be no healthy environment where there is a weak economy, however, because wherever people live from hand to mouth, they will strip the environment in order to survive. We cannot maintain a strong economy in a depleted environment: when natural resources are gone, there will be nothing to support economic growth.

In a very real sense the future of our nation depends on our farmers and ranchers, who must preserve the environment and at the same time guarantee a sustainable food supply. Everything that happens affects everything else. If the United States cannot feed its own people, those countries from which we import agricultural products may find it necessary to destroy more acres of tropical rain forest.

South central Florida is a unique land. It is not the tropics, yet it teems with tropical and subtropical flora and fauna, many of which can't be found anywhere else on earth. It supports huge bustling urban areas, and within only a few miles of them, some of our nation's largest cattle ranches. It has launched men into space, yet it is one of America's last wild frontiers.

We still have the opportunity to preserve these diverse elements. Florida's cities and farms and ranches, humans and cattle and wildlife, tourists and retirees and space-age technology, still have the potential to coexist in harmony.

But the challenge must be approached as a whole and not piecemeal. And we humans, the environment's most intelligent and powerful inhabitants, must learn to live with our surroundings and to become more willing to accept them and share them with others.

To make Adams Ranch more accessible
to bird-watchers, tourists, and nature
lovers, Florida Ranch Tours was orga-
nized as a company to offer tours of the
ranch. Guests can enjoy refreshments in
a chickee or tree house while they
watch wildlife in a natural setting.

Index

If you enjoyed reading this book, here are some other Pineapple Press titles you might enjoy as well. To request our complete catalog or to place an order, write to Pineapple Press, P.O. Box 3899, Sarasota, Florida 34230, or call 1-800-PINEAPL (746-3275).

FLORIDA FICTION:
A Land Remembered by Patrick Smith. Three generations of the MacIveys, a Florida family battling the hardships of the frontier, rise from a dirt-poor cracker life to the wealth and standing of real estate tycoons. ISBN: 0-910923-12-4 (hb); 1-56164-116-2 (pb)

CRACKER WESTERNS:
Guns of the Palmetto Plains by Rick Tonyan. As the Civil War explodes over Florida, Tree Hooker dodges Union soldiers and Florida outlaws to drive cattle to feed the starving Confederacy. ISBN: 1-56164-061-1 (hb); 1-56164-070-0 (pb)

Riders of the Suwannee by Lee Gramling. Tate Barkley returns to 1870s Florida just in time to come to the aid of a young widow and her children as they fight to save their homestead from outlaws. ISBN: 1-56164-046-8 (hb); 1-56164-043-3 (pb)

Thunder on the St. Johns by Lee Gramling. Riverboat gambler Chance Ramsay teams up with the family of young Josh Carpenter and the trapper's daughter Abby Macklin to combat greedy outlaws seeking to destroy the dreams of honest homesteaders. ISBN: 1-56164-064-6 (hb); 156164-080-8 (pb)

Trail from St. Augustine by Lee Gramling. A young trapper, a crusty ex-sailor, and an indentured servant girl fleeing a cruel master join forces to cross the Florida wilderness in search of buried treasure and a new life. ISBN: 1-56164-047-6 (hb); 1-56164-042-5 (pb)

FLORIDA REGIONAL INTEREST:
Classic Cracker by Ronald W. Haase. A study of Florida's wood-frame vernacular architecture that traces the historical development of the regional building style, including single-pens, double-pens, dog trots, and shotgun houses. ISBN: 1-56164-013-1 (hb); 1-56164-014-X (pb)

Florida Horse Owner's Field Guide, Second Edition by Marty Marth. Accurate, easy-to-read guide to selecting, caring for, and enjoying a horse in Florida. Includes updated state park, riding trail, and national riding club information. ISBN: 1-56164-154-5 (pb)

Florida Portrait: A Pictorial History of Florida by Jerrell Shofner. An in-depth reference—packed with hundreds of rare photographs—that chronicles Florida's history from the earliest Spanish explorers and Native American cultures to the space age and rampant population growth in the late twentieth century. ISBN: 1-56164-121-9 (pb)

Florida's Past, Volumes 1, 2, and 3 by Gene Burnett. Collected essays from Burnett's "Florida's Past" columns in *Florida Trend* magazine, plus some original writings not found elsewhere. Burnett's easygoing style and his sometimes surprising choice of topics make history good reading. ISBN: *Vol. 1* 0-910923-27-2 (hb); 1-56164-115-4 (pb) *Vol. 2* 0-910923-59-0 (hb); 1-56164-139-1 (pb) *Vol. 3* 0-910923-84-1 (hb); 1-56164-117-0 (pb)

Alto Adams Jr. is a third-generation Floridian who graduated from the University of Florida in 1948 and began managing Adams Ranch that same year. He was president of the Florida Cattlemen's Association in 1959, founded the International Braford Association in 1969, and in 1991 received both the National Cattlemen's Association's Stewardship Award and the Florida Cattlemen's Association's Environmental Award. He served as chairman of the Indian River Community College Foundation for many years and is founder and chairman of the Florida Wildlife and Livestock Foundation.